AWARD HANDBOOK

4TH Edition

This Handbook provides guidance for Award Leaders and helpers

The Duke of Edinburgh's Award
Gulliver House, Madeira Walk, WINDSOR, Berkshire SL4 1EU
Tel: 01753 727400 Fax: 01753 810666
www.theaward.org

The International Award Association

The Duke of Edinburgh's Award subscribes to the following declaration of principle of the International Award Association:

'The Award concept is one of individual challenge. It presents to young people a balanced, non-competitive programme of voluntary activities which encourages personal discovery and growth, self-reliance, perseverance, responsibility to themselves and service to their community'

The Fundamental Principles
'The criterion for gaining an Award is individual improvement through persistence and achievement, taking into account the participant's initial capabilities and without any element of competition between participants.

Participation is entirely voluntary and the individual participant has a completely free choice in the selection of the locally available options within the four Sections specified.

There is no discrimination against participation on grounds of sex, race, religion or political affiliation.'

Photographic Credits

The majority of photographs in this book were taken by the following Halina/Fuji Bursary Photographers:

Fergus Burnett, John D McFarlene, Tony French, Jennie Hills, Tom Pietrasik, Paul Smith and Tobias Wilson.

The Halina/Fuji Bursary has allowed the Award to employ young photographers on one year contracts since 1993. It has been made possible through the support of Halina Marketing, Fuji Photo Film, Standard Photographic, Amateur Photographer, Merlin Expo International, Minolta and Nikon.

Other photographers are used with permission from Joe Cornish.

Buckingham Palace

Introduction From His Royal Highness The Duke of Edinburgh KG,KT

Young people growing up in this modern complicated world have many difficulties to face, and opportunities for personal achievement are often limited. At the same time, parents, teachers, voluntary organisation leaders and employers, who recognise their responsibilities towards young people, also have their problems.

This scheme is intended to help both the young as well as those who are concerned for their welfare. The object is to provide an introduction to worthwhile leisure activities and voluntary service; as a challenge to the individual to discover the satisfaction of achievement and as a guide for those people and organisations who would like to encourage the development of their younger fellow citizens.

I hope that all those who take part in this scheme will find an added purpose and pleasure in their lives. I am quite sure that all those who help to run it will gain that special sense of satisfaction which comes from helping others to discover hidden abilities and to overcome a challenge.

Philip

Contents **Page**

Chapter 1 The Award

1.1 Aim of the Award

The Duke of Edinburgh's Award aims to provide an enjoyable, challenging and rewarding programme of personal development for young people, which is of the highest quality and the widest reach.

1.2 Key Principles

It is essential that everyone involved in the Award, whether as a participant or Leader, shares a common understanding of the principles which underpin all aspects of the Award's delivery. These key principles are:

Non-Competitive
The Award is a personal challenge and not a competition against others. Each participant's programme is tailor-made to reflect the individual starting point, abilities and interests.

Available to All
With a commitment to equal opportunities, the Award Programme is available to all young people who choose to take up its challenge.

Voluntary
Young people make a free choice to enter the programme and commit their own time to undertake the activities.

Flexible
Young people design their own programme, which can be geared to their choice and personal circumstances and also to local provision. They may enter for whichever level of Award best suits them, and may take as long as they wish to complete an Award.

Balanced
By choosing activities in each of four different Sections (five at Gold), participants undertake a balanced and wide ranging programme.

Progressive
At each level, the Award Programme demands more time and an increasing degree of commitment and responsibility from the participant.

Achievement Focused

Before starting an activity, young people are encouraged to set their own goals. If they aim for those goals and show improvement, they will achieve their Award.

Marathon, not a Sprint

The Award demands persistence and commitment and cannot be completed in a short burst of enthusiasm. Participants may want to continue with activities beyond the minimum time requirements set out for each level of the Award.

Personal Development

The Award is a programme of personal and social development. The value to young people is dependent on personal commitment, the learning process and the quality of the experience.

Enjoyable

Young people and helpers should find participation enjoyable and satisfying.

1.3 Benefits to Participants

In taking part, participants develop:

- self-belief
- self-confidence
- a sense of identity
- independence – of thought and action
- a sense of responsibility
- an awareness of their potential
- new talents and abilities
- an understanding of strengths and weaknesses
- the ability to plan and use time effectively
- the ability to learn from and give to others in the community
- new relationships
- skills including problem solving, presentation and communication
- the ability to lead and work as part of a team

Chapter 2 General Conditions

2.1 Delegation, Flexibility and Trust

The Award operates through a system of delegated responsibility. Operating Authorities are licensed by the Award to operate the Programme and to maintain its quality and standards. This responsibility is then delegated to Award Leaders and, through other helpers, to participants.

Following adequate briefing, Leaders and helpers are given the flexibility to make informed decisions and are entrusted to run the Award in line with its philosophy, principles and conditions.

2.2 Levels and Sections

There are three separate Awards - Bronze, Silver and Gold with different minimum starting ages and periods of participation. At each level there are four Sections:

— **Service** - to encourage service to individuals and the community

— **Skills** - to encourage the discovery and development of personal interests and social and practical skills

— **Physical Recreation** - to encourage participation and improvement in physical activity

— **Expeditions** - to encourage a spirit of adventure and discovery

There is an additional requirement at Gold level:

— **Residential Project** - to broaden experience through involvement with others in a residential setting

2.3 Choice

Participants can either choose from the lists in each Section in chapter 3, or develop their own programme to meet the principles of that Section and their own personal interests, aspirations and goals.

Participants are encouraged to explore and pursue different initiatives which may be new to them, or to further develop existing interests and skills.

Operating Authorities have overall responsibility for monitoring the quality of participants' experience and safety. As such, they may have additional guidelines and safety requirements relating to particular activities. New programmes and activities can be developed in consultation with the Award Leader and Operating Authority.

Programme guidelines for many of these activities are provided in the Award's *Programmes File*.

2.4 Overall Time Requirements

Participants are encouraged to work at their own pace but it should be noted that the minimum periods of participation are:

Level	Minimum period of participation by:	
	Direct entrants	Previous Award holders
Bronze	6 months	
Silver	12 months	6 months
Gold	18 months	12 months

The term **direct entrants** refers to those entering the Award at either Silver or Gold, and who do not hold the previous level of Award.

2.5 Timescales for the Sections of the Award

Bronze Award

Service	Skills	Physical Recreation	Expeditions
3 months	3 months	3 months	Plan, prepare for and undertake a 2 day, 1 night venture

All participants must undertake a further 3 months in either the Service, Skills or Physical Recreation Section

Silver Award

Service	Skills	Physical Recreation	Expeditions
6 months	One Section for 6 months and the other Section for 3 months		Plan, prepare for and undertake a 3 day, 2 night venture

Direct entrants must undertake a further 6 months in either the Service or the longer of the Skills or Physical Recreation Sections

Gold Award

Service	Skills	Physical Recreation	Expeditions	Residential
12 months	One Section for 12 months and the other Section for 6 months		Plan, prepare for and undertake a 4 day, 3 night venture	Undertake a shared activity in a residential setting away from home for 5 days and 4 nights

Direct entrants must undertake a further 6 months in either the Service or the longer of the Skills or Physical Recreation Sections

Participants should decide which Section to undertake for the longer period at the beginning of their Award, however this decision can be reviewed once the participant has begun the activities.

In the Service, Skills and Physical Recreation Sections the minimum time requirements are expressed in months, during which there should be regular commitment averaging at least an hour a week.

Participants are encouraged to continue activities beyond the minimum time requirements of the Award in order to meet their personal objectives.

2.6 Age Requirements

Age Range

The age range for the Programme is from the 14th to the 25th birthday.

Minimum Ages

The minimum ages of entry are as follows:

Bronze	14 years
Silver	15 years
Gold	16 years

Subject to the above minimum ages, entry into the Programme may be at Bronze, Silver or Gold level.

Discretion is given to Operating Authorities to permit those who are too young to enter the Bronze Award **but who are part of a larger group aged 14 years and above to make a start with their friends.**

- this discretion is primarily intended for those who plan their activities on a group basis
- Group Leaders must be satisfied that participants are sufficiently mature to undertake the Bronze Programme

Operating Authorities may permit those who have completed the Bronze Award to make a start on the Silver Award before their 15th birthday without imposing an artificial delay.

No activity can count towards the Gold Award before the 16th birthday.

Age of Completion

Participants must continue their involvement with the Award until they reach the minimum ages for completion which are:

Bronze	All entrants	14 ½
Silver	Bronze Award holders Direct entrants	15 ½ 16
Gold	Silver Award holders Direct entrants	17 17 ½

Maximum Ages

The upper age limit for all Awards is the 25th birthday, by which time all activities which count for an Award must be completed.

Extension

Extensions to the upper age limit can only be considered where illness, accident or unavoidable circumstances make it impossible to complete an Award by the age of 25. In these circumstances requests are to be referred, in writing, by Operating Authorities to the Award Secretary, Regional Officer or Award Head Office, as appropriate, for consideration. If the application is successful, extra time will be allowed which must not be further exceeded.

2.7 Entry into the Award

Young people enter the Award when they enrol with an Operating Authority.

2.8 Activities Prior to Entry

Activities followed prior to entry into the Award may count if undertaken:

- during the preceding three months, or
- with an Access Organisation (see page 82)

and in accordance with the Award's principles

The minimum age requirements for the level of Award and the conditions of the appropriate Section must be met.

2.9 What and When

The Award is essentially a programme of activities undertaken during free or personal time. The Programme should be voluntarily undertaken at times when participants have freedom of choice as to whether they participate or not (i.e. personal or non-directed time).

Activities can be vocational or non-vocational.

Those activities pursued partly within directed curriculum or work time can count where:

- the participant demonstrates a substantial contribution of personal time and voluntary effort
- the activities are not followed for examination or career advancement purposes

2.10 Entrance Packs and Record Books

An *Entrance Pack* and *Record Book* are normally issued to participants by an Operating Authority on enrolment in the Award. The *Entrance Pack* contains background information on the Award, ideas of activities for each Section and advice on planning activities and recording progress and achievement.

The *Record Book* forms a record of progress and outcomes through the Award, verified by the individuals who have carried out the review and assessment in each Section.

It represents the experiences and achievements of a young person and remarks by assessors should relate to the individual and be positive and encouraging.

The start date (briefing) and finish date (review) for each Section should be entered together with details of any training courses attended or qualifications gained.

In the event of a young person not meeting the requirements, the reasons should be discussed with the assessor and no entry made in the *Record Book* until the requirements have been satisfactorily fulfilled.

Participants should be encouraged to review and record their personal acheivements and comments in the *Record Book*.

2.11 Starting the Next Level of Award

Participants should be encouraged to complete all Sections of one Award before embarking on the next. However, they may start on a Section of the next level of Award prior to completing the previous Award provided that they:

- obtain a *Record Book* for the next Award
- have completed that Section in the previous Award
- have reached the minimum age of entry for the next Award
- are not working on all three Awards at the same time

2.12 Lost Record Books

Lost *Record Books* may be replaced and previous entries endorsed by the Operating Authority. Lost certificates and badges may be replaced on application to the Operating Authority and, at Gold level, to the appropriate Award Office. Recipients must provide evidence that the Award was granted and a small charge may be made.

2.13 Changing Award Groups

When a participant leaves a Group or moves to a new area, the Award Officer of the new Operating Authority should be able to put the participant in touch with the nearest Award Group. Details of Operating Authorities can be obtained from the appropriate UK Award Office. Once the participant has been linked to a new Group, the Group details should be amended in the front of the *Record Book*.

Contact information is included in the *Entrance Pack*, the *Award Journal* magazine and on the Award's web site *www.theaward.org* The International Award Association is able to provide details of the relevant Award contacts in other countries.

All entries in a *Record Book,* authenticated by the previous Operating Authority, should be honoured by the new one.

2.14 Authorisation of Awards

The *Record Book* should be sent to the appropriate official in the Operating Authority who will authorise the Award. A participant qualifies for an Award when the Operating Authority or Award Office confirms that the relevant conditions have been met, based on the information recorded in the *Record Book*.

At Gold level, a *Gold Award form* needs to be completed and signed by the participant and Leader and sent to the Operating Authority who, in turn, will forward it to the appropriate Award Secretary, Regional Officer or Head Office as appropriate, for final confirmation.

2.15 Helpers in the Award

Helpers are all those who contribute to the Award Group and support participants in any way. They may be volunteers or paid.

Helpers may carry out one or more of the following roles:

Award Leader	Supervisor
Assistant Leader	Mentor
Instructor	Assessor

These roles are defined in the Glossary on page 92.

AWARD

3

Service
Skills
Physical Recreation
Expeditions
Residential Project

Chapter 3 SECTIONS

3.1 Choosing Activities

Participants choose the activities they wish to pursue in each Section, taking into consideration local availability and cost.

3.2 Degree of Challenge

Through the Award young people learn self-reliance and it is the Award's aim to empower them to take responsibility for their own programmes and, having gained confidence and experience, to apply it to other aspects of their lives. However, the degree of challenge should not be so daunting as to present unrealistic expectations and reduce, rather than build confidence. Leaders and other helpers, therefore, should ensure that the challenge is appropriate to the young person's ability and maturity.

3.3 Taking a Break

Young people are able to take a break from participating in activities counting towards their Award when circumstances intervene, for example during exam periods.

3.4 Changing Activities

Where circumstances necessitate, participants may choose to change the activity undetaken once in each Section at any time during participation. Both should be recorded in the *Record Book*.

3.5 Balanced Programme

The Award is designed to allow flexibility but, to preserve its framework and integrity, young people should be encouraged to undertake a balanced programme of activities and to consider the option of following different types of activities in each Section. Where an activity is listed in, for example, the Skills Section, it should not be undertaken in the Physical Recreation Section.

SERVICE

MOUNTAIN
PATTERDALE
RESCUE

Service

Aim of the Service Section

To encourage service to individuals and to the community.

The Principles

This Section is based on the belief that members of a community have a responsibility to each other and voluntary help is needed.

Young people should identify the voluntary service required to gain some knowledge of the needs of those whom they are assisting and then receive briefing and training in the skills required to give that service. The value of participation in the Service Section comes from training, giving practical service and appreciating the needs of the community.

Benefits to Young People

Although the specific benefits depend on the choice of activity, the Service Section should provide opportunities to:

- **make a personal contribution** by dedicating free time to giving service to the community
- **appreciate the needs of others and contribute to their well-being** by working with and for people with whom young people would not normally come into contact
- **trust and be trusted**
- **understand personal strengths and weaknesses** by reviewing their performance in briefing and training sessions
- **increase self-esteem** by receiving positive feedback and learning to appreciate the value of making a personal contribution
- **overcome prejudice and fears** through building new relationships and developing an empathy with others
- **generate positive action in the community** by identifying and undertaking worthwhile service projects which benefit the local or wider community or the environment
- **accept responsibility** through a personal commitment to an individual, organisation, group or community

Requirements

Participants are required to train for and give service to others. Consideration should first be given to the proposed form of practical service to be followed and then to the training required so that the service can be undertaken with competence and insight.

Depending on the form of service chosen, this training could range from an outline briefing session to a specialised training course or qualification.

The time requirements for this Section are set out on page 7.

- there is flexibility as to how the hours are spent within the total time span, as long as there is regular involvement throughout, averaging at least an hour a week
- for forms of service requiring a training course or qualification, the minimum time requirements include the time spent in training and the time spent in practical service

The Process

There are four stages in the Service Section:

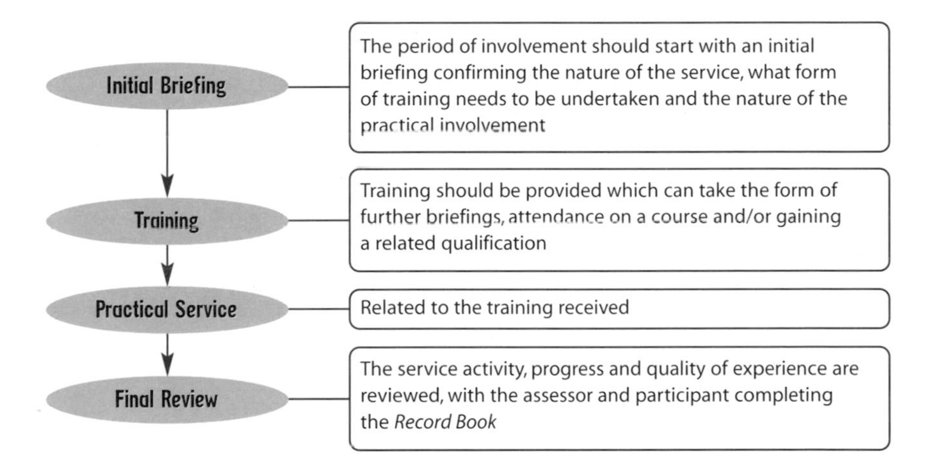

Initial Briefing

The initial briefing should help the participant to confirm that they have made the right choice of service and clarify the commitment. Through discussion between the participant and the supervisor, mentor or assessor, the initial briefing should cover the following areas:

- establish the nature of the service to be undertaken i.e. the practical task, commitment required etc.
- define and understand the purpose of the service - the needs of the individual, organisation or community
- any necessary safety or legal requirements should be identified and followed
- define the role of the participant by discussing and agreeing an individual programme, goals and expectations
- establish what training is required, such as health and safety, legal factors, skills etc.
- establish a system for regular supervision and monitoring and agree the process for review, evaluation and assessment

Training

A participant's choice may require a course of specialised training, and the course instructor should be aware that it is being undertaken as part of the Award Programme. On completion of the course or attainment of the relevant qualification, the course instructor or examiner should sign the participant's *Record Book.*

For courses without qualifications, the structure and format of training will vary depending on the agency or organisation involved and the resources available. The course should have an emphasis on practical sessions, supported with additional briefing sessions during these practical sessions. Dates and details of training undertaken should be recorded by the participant for use in the final review.

Where a form of service has a training course or qualification, then this should be followed. Where it is not available or appropriate the Operating Authority may authorise adaptations. Details on qualifications can be found in the *Programmes File.*

Practical Service

- all participants must undertake practical service following their training
- the practical service should relate to the training undertaken, providing the opportunity to apply the knowledge gained on the course, and may be undertaken either as a group, or on an individual basis
- minimum age restrictions and legal insurance requirements may apply to some service opportunities and must always be observed

Instruction, Supervision and Assessment

Instruction and assessment should be undertaken by individuals who are knowledgeable, experienced or qualified in the chosen activity. They should be acceptable to the Operating Authority, relate easily and effectively to young people and have the necessary expertise and enthusiasm to guide and encourage participants in their efforts.

The supervisor, assessor or mentor should monitor the practical service throughout and facilitate opportunities to:

- discuss progress
- clarify and provide guidance
- support participants in resolving any problems
- help participants to learn from their experiences
- agree goals and discuss expectations for the next phase of practical service
- review the choice of service if necessary

For Forms of Service Requiring a Training Course or Qualification

It is essential that both the instructor and the assessor are qualified people approved by the appropriate governing body and the Operating Authority. The instructor and the assessor may be the same person, but in some cases independent assessment may be desirable.

The assessment of practical service should confirm that participants have applied the knowledge gained during the period of training and have shown reliability, competence and an understanding of the need for the service given.

Final Review

This should:

- reflect on the need for the service
- review the benefits to the organisation concerned and/or the wider community
- enable the participant to identify what they have gained from, and the quality of their experience

After the review, the participant's *Record Book* is completed and signed by the assessor with the participant adding comments if they wish to do so.

Choice

Participants can use the following list of ideas or, alternatively, they can develop their own programme to meet community needs. Participants are encouraged to explore and pursue different and interesting initiatives.

The choice of service should reflect a young person's individual interests, talents and capabilities but also be challenging and may build on previous experiences. Service programmes are currently available either in the *Programmes File*, on the Award website *www.theaward.org* or from the relevant UK Award Office.

It would be helpful if new programmes produced were forwarded to the appropriate Award Office to enable new ideas to be publicised.

Norton
POLICE

Ideas

People in the Community

- Assisting at day centres, creches, playschemes
- Assisting children and young people at risk
- Award Leadership
- Child Care
- Dance Leadership
- Helping children and young people with special needs
- Learning Support
- Mountain/Expedition Leadership
- Religious Education Leadership
- Sports Leadership
- Uniformed Youth Organisation Leadership
- Visiting Children in Care
- Youth Work
- Peer Support Projects
- Community Care
- Assisting with community based charities
- Child Care
- Community Support for elderly or disabled people
- First Aid
- Helping at clubs, homes and day centres
- Home Nursing
- Support for elderly or disabled people
- Visiting elderly or disabled people

Emergency Services

- Ambulance Service
- Assistance with Emergency Service charities
- Civil Aid
- Coastguard Services
- Fire Services
- Lifeboat Service
- Police Service

Environmental Service

- Assisting with a conservation charity or project
- Assisting with an animal or environmental charity
- Care for Animals

Fundraising

- Fundraising for a charity or project
- Fundraising for an animal or environmental charity
- Fundraising for children's charities
- Fundraising for community based charities
- Fundraising for emergency charities
- Fundraising for rescue services
- Fundraising for safety charities

Rescue Service

- Assisting rescue service charities
- Canoe Lifeguard
- Cave Rescue
- Mountain Rescue
- Rescue Coxswain (RYA)
- Royal Life Saving Society
- Surf Lifesaving

Safety Training

- Accident Prevention
- Assisting with a safety charity
- Cycle Proficiency Instruction
- Road Safety

SKILLS

SKILLS
Skills

Aim of the Skills Section

To encourage the discovery and development of practical and social skills and personal interests.

The Principles

This Section should encourage young people to pursue activities within a wide range of practical, cultural and social environments. The Skills Section offers young people a wide choice depending upon their personal preferences, abilities and the opportunities available. The skill may be an existing interest or something entirely new.

Skills

Benefits to Young People

Although the specific benefits to young people depend on the choice made, the Skills Section should provide opportunities to:

- **develop practical and social skills** by working alongside enthusiastic individuals who share their skills and knowledge
- **meet new people**
- **organise and manage time**
- **discover how to research information** through communication with the instructor or mentor, using the internet, libraries and other resources, making appropriate contacts in the community and identifying other sources of help and guidance
- **set and respond to a challenge** by developing an existing interest or trying something new
- **work with others** to build relationships, gain benefit from their knowledge, appreciate their skills and to share a mutual interest
- **enjoy sharing** an activity with adults and peers
- **discover new talents**

Requirements

Participants should follow an activity and show progression and sustained interest over a period of time, leading to a deeper knowledge of the subject and the attainment of an increased degree of skill.

The time requirements for this Section are set out on page 7.

The Process

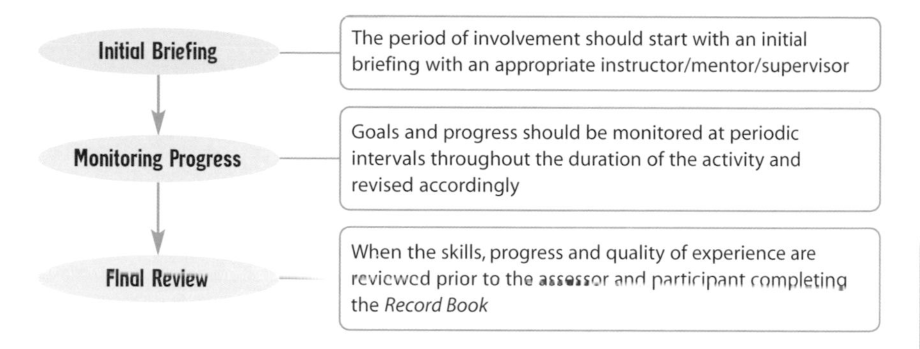

Initial Briefing

The initial briefing should help the participant confirm the choice of skill and clarify the commitment. The start date for the skill should be at the date of the initial briefing and the finish date at the final review when the *Record Book* is completed.

The participant may follow the skill independently or as a member of a group. Knowledge and experience may be acquired by attending a course or by individual enquiry.

Through discussion between the participant and the instructor, supervisor or mentor, the briefing should cover the following areas:

- discuss the activity to be pursued i.e. the practical task, commitment required and the benefits to the participant
- discuss and agree a programme incorporating individual goals and ambitions
- identify and follow any necessary safety or legal requirements
- arrange necessary support or training related to health and safety, skills and awareness
- establish a system for support and agree the process for evaluation and assessment
- discuss how progress is to be recorded and the format of the final review
- consider the potential use of planning and recording pages within the Entrance Pack
- arrange the dates and times of meetings

Monitoring Progress

The participant should meet with their instructor, supervisor or mentor at regular intervals to:

- discuss progress
- clarify and provide guidance
- resolve any problems
- reflect on progress and learn from experience
- reaffirm goals and discuss expectations for the next phase
- review the choice of activity if necessary

Instruction and Assessment

Instruction and assessment should be undertaken by individuals who are knowledgeable and experienced in the chosen activity. The instructor and the assessor may be the same person, but in some cases independent assessment may be desirable. They should be acceptable to the Operating Authority, relate easily and effectively to young people and have the necessary expertise and enthusiasm to guide and encourage participants in their efforts.

A young person completes this Section when the assessor, after consultation with the instructor where applicable, is satisfied that:

- the minimum timescales for participation have been met in free time
- the skill has been regularly followed for the required time
- genuine effort and individual progress have been made within the young person's capability

Final Review

- Each individual is to be assessed throughout the required period on effort, perseverance and achievement
- Group activities are to be assessed with regard to each individual's contribution to planning, execution and completion
- Participants should have the opportunity to review the quality of their experience in this Section
- On conclusion of the Review the participant's *Record Book* should be completed and signed by the assessor with the participant adding their comments if they so desire

Selecting a Skill

A list of established skills programmes is shown on page 32. This list is not exhaustive, and guidelines on how to develop new programmes can be found in the *Programmes File*. The choice should reflect a young person's individual interests, talents and capabilities and build on previous experiences. More information and advice is available on each programme in the *Programmes File*, or from the Award web site: *www.theaward.org*

To help with choosing an activity for the Skills Section, the chart in the *Programmes File* could be of assistance.

Activities appearing in a different Section of the Award should only be pursued under that Section e.g. yoga is regarded as a Physical Recreation option.

New Skills Programmes

Using the guidelines in the *Programmes File*, a proposed programme should be drawn up by the young person and/or a person knowledgeable in the activity, to meet the principles of the Section.

The programme should:

- focus on a specific activity or theme, rather than comprise a series of 'tasters'
- reflect the ability and experience of the young person
- be progressive and allow achievement to be demonstrated over a period of time
- contain appropriate safe working practices and legal requirements

IDENTICOLOR
hilmnopqrux
CENTURY ENGLISH MS.
SLIGHTLY

Choice

The Skills Section provides opportunities to study and develop social and life skills, and explore health-related issues. Activities may be vocational provided they are undertaken in personal, non-directed time.

The following alphabetical list contains examples of activities which have been undertaken by participants to date. Further details on these examples and other activities can be found in the *Programmes File*, on the Award web site or obtained from the appropriate Award Office.

- Agriculture – farming
- Aircraft – study of, recognition, flying, construction, restoration
- Animals – keeping, breeding, studying, racing, handling
- Archaeology
- Architectural Appreciation – contempory, historic, church
- Art and Design – painting, drawing, etching, calligraphy,
- Enameling
- Astronautics
- Astronomy
- Audio Broadcast – radio, DJ-ing
- Baton Twirling and Majorettes
- Bellringing
- Billiards, Snooker and Pool
- Boat Building – construction, restoration
- Book Binding
- Camp Equipment – construction
- Candlemaking
- Cars – engineering and construction
- Cars – maintenance
- Cars – roadskills
- Casualty Simulation
- Chess
- Choirs
- Circus Skills
- Citizenship politics and democracy
- Coastal Navigation
- Coins – collecting, study of
- Committee Procedures
- Communication with people who have a hearing impairment
- Communication with people who have a visual impairment
- Conjuring and Magic
- Conservation
- Consumer Information
- Cookery
- Criminology
- Cycle Maintenance
- Darts
- Debating and Public Speaking
- Drugs and Peer Education
- Fantasy Games
- Fashion – design, study, dressmaking
- Film and Video Production
- Fishing
- Floral Art
- Furniture – making, restoration

Gardening	Life Skills	Performing Arts
Geology	Literacy – skills and literature	Performing Arts Appreciation
Genealogy	Magazine and Newsletter Production	Photography
Geometrical and Technical Drawing	Marksmanship	Plants – study of, growing
Glasswork	Metalwork – pewter work	Pottery and Ceramics
Handbell Ringing	Meteorology/weather study	Printing – screen, fabric, lino, lithography
Health and Style	Model Construction	Radio Construction
Historical Period Renactment	Money Matters	Religion
IT – use of standard packages, design of systems, web site design	Mosaic	Rug Making
Interior design – furnishing and decorating, DIY, soft furnishing	Motorcycles and Mopeds – roadskills	Sculpture – clay, stone, wood
Jewellery	Motorcycle, Mopeds and Scooters – maintenance	Sport Appreciation
Journalism	Motor Sport – motor cross, powerboating, jet skiing	Sport Officiating
Karting	Music Appreciation	Stamp Collecting
Kite Construction and Flying	Music Playing	Table and Indoor Games
Languages	Natural History	Taxidermy
Leatherwork	Needlecrafts	Wine Making
Library and Information Skills	Papercrafts	Woodwork
		Young Engineers
		Young Enterprises
		Zoology

Note: It would be helpful if new programmes produced were forwarded to Award Head Office so that the number of requests for a new activities may be monitored and the most popular published.

PHYSICAL RECREATION

Aim of the Physical Recreation Section

To encourage participation and improvement in physical activity.

The Principles

This Section offers a wide range of programmes in the belief that:

- involvement in some form of enjoyable physical activity is essential for physical well-being
- a lasting sense of achievement and satisfaction is derived from meeting a physical challenge
- sports are enjoyable in themselves and can lead to the establishment of a lasting active lifestyle
- young people should have the opportunity to make a choice, then discuss and agree a personal programme of participation and achievement

Benefits to Young People

The Physical Recreation Section should provide opportunities to:

- **enjoy keeping fit** by choosing an activity which is in itself enjoyable, and which leads to the establishment of a lasting, active lifestyle
- **improve fitness** by taking part in a physical activity on a regular basis
- **discover new abilities**
- **raise self-esteem** through improvement of performance and reaching the minimum requirements
- **extend personal goals** by involvement and sustained interest
- **set and respond to a challenge** by extending physical fitness and performance
- **experience a sense of achievement** from meeting a physical challenge

Requirements

Assessed participation in an activity and achievement of individual progress.

- achievement should be measured by regular participation and improvement in personal performance over the minimum period of months
- each participant should discuss and agree their programme with their instructor or assessor, including the content and appropriate goals. A means of measuring performance and/or progress could be the attainment of a national governing body award or standard
- participation should be undertaken in accordance with any national governing body safety requirements and, where possible, through clubs or organisations approved by the relevant governing body

The time requirements for this Section are set out on page 7.

The Process

Initial Briefing	The period of involvement should start with an initial briefing with an appropriate instructor/assessor
Monitoring Progress	Goals and progress should be monitored throughout the duration of the Section and adapted accordingly
Final Review	When the activity, progress (evidence of standards gained etc.) and quality of experience are reviewed. Prior to both the assessor and participant completing the *Record Book*

Initial Briefing

The initial briefing should help the participant confirm that they have made the right choice and clarify the commitment. Through discussion between the participant and instructor, assessor or mentor the briefing may cover the following areas:

- discuss the choice, the commitment required and the potential benefits
- discuss and agree an individual programme, incorporating goals and ambitions
- establish a system for support and monitoring and agree the process for evaluation and assessment
- where possible, the progress and performance should be measured against the relevant national governing body standard

Monitoring Progress

The participant should meet with their instructor or assessor at regular intervals to discuss progress. The instructor or assessor should:

- help to resolve any issues
- encourage reflection on performance and learning from experience
- reaffirm goals and discuss expectations for the next phase
- note national governing body awards or standards attained, where appropriate, and review performance against these
- review the choice of activity if necessary

Final Review

Instruction and assessment should be undertaken by those who hold the appropriate governing body or professional qualifications. They should also be acceptable to the Operating Authority, relate easily and effectively to young people and have the necessary expertise and enthusiasm to guide and encourage participants in their efforts.

The instructor and the assessor may be the same person, but in some cases independent assessment may be desirable.

To provide a 'benchmark' for monitoring and assessing progress, participants should be encouraged to attain or work towards national governing body awards or standards where available.

Assessment is a continuing process throughout the period of participation and the following areas could be considered when undertaking the final review:

- effort
- application
- technique
- skill
- tactics
- improvement in fitness and achievement
- knowledge of the relevant rules and safety regulations
- quality of experience

On completion of the review, the participant's *Record Book* should be completed and signed by the assessor with the participant adding their own comments if they wish.

New Programmes

Participants can develop their own programme to meet the principles of the Section, provided that the activity:

- has a national governing body which is recognised by UK Sport, the British Sports Trust or the relevant home country sports council
- has Operating Authority approval

Operating Authorities have overall responsibility for monitoring the quality of the participant's experience and their safety. As such, they may have additional guidelines and safety requirements relating to particular activities.

TOP END

Choice

The Physical Recreation Section offers young people a wide choice depending upon their personal preferences, abilities and the opportunities available. The young person may already be involved in the activity or the choice could be something entirely new.

If the choice of activity is not listed, the programme must be confirmed in advance by the Operating Authority.

The alphabetical list contains examples which have been undertaken to date. Further details and other activities can be found in the *Programmes File,* on the Award web site or obtained from the appropriate Award Office.

Aerobics	Dragon Boat Racing	Netball
Archery	Fencing	Octopushing
Athletics	Fitness Activities – aerobics aquarobics, multi-gym, jogging	Orienteering
Badminton		Parachuting/Sky Diving
Baseball	Fives	Paragliding
Basketball	Football and Gaelic Association Football	Pentaque
BMX Racing		Physical Achievement
Boccia	Golf	Polo
Bowling	Gymnastics	Real Tennis
Camogie	Hang Gliding	Riding
Canoe Polo	Hockey – Field, Ice, Roller, Street	Rounders
Canoeing		Rowing and Sculling
Carriage Driving	Hurling	Rugby League Football
Caving and Potholing	Judo	Rugby Union Football
Climbing	Keep Fit	Running
Cricket	Korfball	Sailing and Windsurfing
Croquet	Lacrosse	Sand and Land Yachting
Cross Country Running	Medau Rhythmic Movement	Skating – Ice, Roller
Curling	Modern Biathlon, Pentathlon, Triathlon	Skiing
Cycling		Skipping
Dance	Mountain Biking	Snowboarding

Squash	Tennis	Water Polo
Stoolball	Tchouk Ball	Water Skiing
Sub Aqua	Trampolining	Weightlifting
Surfing/Body Boarding	Ultimate Flying Disc (Frisbee)	Weight Training
Swimming	Volleyball	Wheelchair Mobility
Table Cricket	Walking	Wrestling
Table Tennis		Yoga

FLEX
C-48

EXPEDITIONS

Expeditions

Aim of the Expeditions Section

To encourage a spirit of adventure and discovery.

The Principles

All ventures involve self-reliant journeying in the countryside or on water, conceived with a purpose and undertaken by the participants' own physical efforts, without motorised assistance. The venture must present the participants with a challenge in terms of purpose, planning and achievement with minimum external intervention.

It is more in keeping with the principles of this Section for participants to choose an environment and form of travel where they can venture with relatively remote supervision rather than undertake a journey which, for safety reasons, requires more direct supervision.

The venture involves:

- enterprise and imagination in concept
- forethought, careful attention to detail and organisational ability in preparation
- preparatory training, both theoretical and practical, leading to the ability to journey safely in the chosen environment
- shared responsibility for the venture, leadership from within the group, self-reliance and co-operation amongst those taking part
- determination in implementation
- a review of the venture in relation to its purpose

Types of Venture

Participants may choose from the following types of venture:

- **Expeditions** which have journeying as their principal component
- **Explorations** which involve less journeying and a greater proportion of time spent on first hand investigations or other specified activities

  At Gold Level there is the additional option of:
- **Other Adventurous Projects** which are of an equally, or more demanding nature but which depart from the specified conditions

Benefits to Young People

Although the challenges are expressed in terms of physical demands, by travelling for a given distance or number of hours, the Award is equally concerned with the development of the individual, teamwork and the social interaction of the group.

This Section should provide opportunities to:

- **plan and execute a task** – requiring attention to detail and organisational ability
- **demonstrate enterprise and imagination** – through a wide choice of ventures
- **work as a member of a team** – all ventures are a group effort
- **respond to a challenge** – both planned and unforeseen
- **develop self-reliance** – through carrying out the qualifying venture unaccompanied
- **develop leadership skills** – members of the group have opportunities to take a leading role during different aspects of the venture
- **recognise the needs and strengths of others** – all are involved in mutual support to complete the venture
- **make decisions and accept the consequences** – groups make real decisions affecting their well-being
- **reflect on personal performance** – through reviewing progress during training and the qualifying venture
- **enjoy and appreciate the countryside** – growing environmental awareness with minimum impact on the countryside

Requirements

The following requirements are for all types of venture.

- all qualifying ventures should have a clearly defined purpose
- on completion, participants review the venture and give an account or presentation related to this purpose
- unaccompanied ventures should take place between the end of March and the end of October
- ventures involve joint planning and preparation by all members of the group
- groups consist of between four and seven young people

- accommodation will be by camping and all equipment must be suitable for the activity and environment in which the venture is to take place
- participants are to be trained in the skills necessary to undertake their planned venture
- participants must undertake sufficient practice journeys to ensure that they are able to journey safely and independently in their chosen environment
- all ventures must be supervised and qualifying ventures assessed by suitably experienced people

Level	Planned Activity*	Walking Expeditions	Cycling, Canoeing HorseRiding, Rowing Expeditions	Sailing Expeditions	Explorations (all modes of travel)
Bronze 2 days, 1 night	Minimum of 6 hours each day	24km/ 15 miles	At least 4 hours journeying each day	12 hours planned activity over the 2 days	At least 5 hours journeying over the 2 days
Silver 3 days, 2 nights	Minimum of 7 hours each day	48km/ 30 miles	At least 5 hours journeying each day	21 hours planned activity over the 3 days	At least 10 hours journeying over the 3 days
Gold 4 days, 3 nights	Minimum of 8 hours each day	80km/ 50 miles	At least 6 hours journeying each day	32 hours planned activity over the 4 days	At least 10 hours journeying over the 4 days

** Planned activity includes journeying, navigation, setting up and striking camp and on tasks related to the purpose of the journey.*

The Process

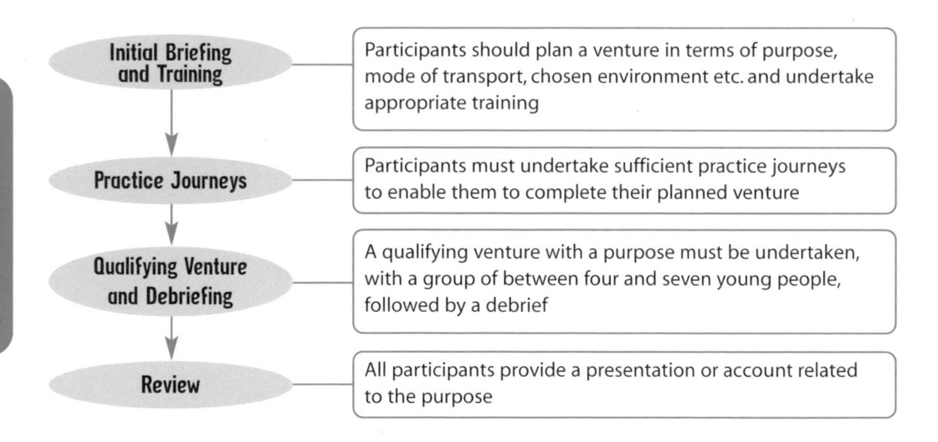

Preparing for the Qualifying Venture

Preparation for the qualifying venture involves:

- an initial briefing to decide on the type of venture
- training in all skills required for the venture
- practice journeys: at least one for each level of Award, and in a wild country environment for qualifying ventures in wild country
- planning by the group

Training

Participants must undertake training in all aspects of the Common Training Syllabus for the appropriate level of Award to enable them to journey safely in the environment in which the qualifying venture will take place. The Common Training Syllabus covers:

- first aid and emergency procedures
- an awareness of risk and health and safety issues
- navigation and route planning
- campcraft, equipment and hygiene
- food and cooking
- Country, Highway and Water Sports Codes (where appropriate)
- observation, recording and purpose
- team building
- proficiency in the mode of travel

The detailed Common Training Syllabus is set out in the *Programmes File* and on the Award's web site *www.theaward.org* The *Expedition Guide* contains practical advice and further details.

Practice Journeys

As part of their training, participants are required to undertake sufficient practice journeys to ensure that they have acquired a level of experience and competence to be able to complete an unaccompanied, self-reliant venture safely.

In order that the Award Leader or instructor has the opportunity to judge the participants' levels of experience and competence, and to give the group the opportunity to work together as a team, **at least one practice journey must be undertaken** at each level of Award.

This practice journey must not be over the same route or in the same vicinity of the route to be used during the qualifying venture. The conditions should be as similar as possible to those anticipated, including daily distance travelled, and should be undertaken in terrain which is equally demanding. Practice journeys at Silver and Gold levels should include two or more nights camping.

For qualifying ventures in wild country this practice journey must be in a wild country environment.

All participants should have an opportunity to experience unaccompanied journeying before undertaking the qualifying venture. Unaccompanied practice journeys must be supervised. If in wild country, the appropriate Wild Country Panel must be informed using the standard *Expedition Notification Form*. These are available from Operating Authorities, Award Offices and The Award Scheme Ltd.

It is recommended that:

- the final practice journey should ideally take place in the same expedition season as the qualifying venture
- practice journeys are not undertaken immediately prior to the qualifying venture as this can make unreasonable demands on the participants and does not allow time to reflect upon or initiate any changes required to their plans

It is not appropriate to prescribe the number of other practice journeys to be undertaken in order to reach the level of competence required. The final practice journey should be seen as the culmination of group work in planning and preparation and in undertaking accompanied practice journeys with the Leader or Instructor before embarking on unaccompanied ventures. The Leader's judgement is crucial in this respect and there are no short cuts where the safety and well-being of the participants is concerned.

Expedition Season

The expedition season for unaccompanied ventures is between the end of March and the end of October and, although specific dates are not prescribed, this period coincides approximately with British Summer Time. This does not preclude appropriately-led training opportunities and practice journeys outside these dates.

The Qualifying Venture

Before the qualifying venture, instructors must certify in the *Record Book* that participants have undergone training in the required skills and have reached a level of competence appropriate to the enterprise being undertaken.

Purpose

The purpose of the venture should be considered in the early planning stages and should relate to the interests and abilities of those taking part.

Participants may wish to focus on:

- practical first-hand observations, investigation or study
- aesthetic appreciation
- literary or historic journeys
- the completion of a physically demanding journey

Further ideas for the purposes of Expeditions and Explorations can be found in the Exploration Resource Pack.

Group Composition

The minimum number in a group at all levels of Award and for all modes of travel is four and the maximum seven. It is not necessary for the entire group to be undertaking the Award or to be under assessment but all must be trained and properly equipped to the same standard as the participants.

Young people who have already qualified in the Expeditions Section at the same or a higher level of the Award are not to be included in the qualifying venture.

Participants being assessed for different levels of Award should not be in the same group i.e. a group under assessment cannot consist of Silver and Gold or Bronze and Silver participants.

For water ventures there must be a minimum of two craft involved in the venture to render mutual support, except for yachts, keelboats and pulling boats which are able to accommodate the whole group.

Accommodation and Catering

Accommodation is by camping. A different campsite must be used each night for Expeditions but, for Explorations, the same campsite may be used on more than one night if the nature of the Exploration necessitates this.

At least one substantial meal should be prepared under camp conditions each day.

Equipment

Clothing, footwear and equipment should be suitable for the activity and the environment in which it is to be used and generally conform to current accepted standards.

The equipment must be capable of resisting the worst weather anticipated since, in the event of a serious deterioration in conditions, safety may well depend on it being able to withstand the prevailing conditions.

The group must carry all equipment and food to be used during the venture. All individuals must always carry the personal emergency equipment listed in the *Programmes File*.

Route Planning

The qualifying venture must take place in surroundings which present an appropriate challenge and are unfamiliar to the participants.

Walking: Routes should make as little use of roads as possible and every effort should be made to avoid villages.

Cycling: Routes should involve minor roads, lanes, tracks and bridleways. Cycling on footpaths is illegal. Villages must be avoided where possible but, because of the distances involved, particularly at Silver and Gold levels, routes may occasionally have to pass through villages. The distance cycled from home to the area of the venture must not be included in the hours of planned activity.

Horse Riding: Routes should involve lanes, tracks and bridleways, avoiding villages where possible.

Bronze	
Land Environment	Ventures should take place in normal rural country which is unfamiliar to the participants
Canoeing and Rowing	Canals, rivers or other inland waterways and lakes
Sailing	Inland waters or estuaries

Silver	
Land Environment	Ventures should take place in normal rural or open country which is unfamiliar to the participants. The environment should make more demands on participants than that used at Bronze level and should represent an intermediate stage between the normal rural environment and wild country. Areas of open country should be used or included where possible
Canoeing and Rowing	Canals, rivers or other inland waterways and lakes in rural areas
Sailing	Inland waters, estuaries or sheltered coastal waters.

Gold	
Land Environment	The environment must be appropriate to the purpose of the venture and the route and the surrounding area must be unfamiliar to the participants
Walking and Cycling	All Expeditions must be in wild country. Explorations may take place in open country
Horse Riding	All Expeditions must take place in wild or open country
Canoeing and Rowing	Rivers, certain inland waterways and lakes. Sheltered coastal waters and estuaries may be used
Sailing	Inland waters, lochs, estuaries or sheltered coastal waters. Yachts may use open sea areas

Bronze and Silver Ventures in more Demanding Surroundings

Where Bronze and Silver ventures are proposed in more demanding surroundings, all participants must be trained and equipped to a standard sufficient to enable them to meet any hazards which they may encounter. The requirements and syllabus at Silver and Gold levels, as appropriate, will need to be utilised. If the venture takes place in wild country, the appropriate Wild Country Panel must be informed (*for further details on Wild Country Panels see Ventures in Wild Country*).

Ventures in Wild Country

Wild country is defined as being areas remote from habitation in which all ventures, for reasons of safety, must be completely self-sufficient. Award ventures should be through rather than over wild country.

The areas defined as wild country in the United Kingdom are shown on the map in the *Programmes File* and in the *Expedition Guide*. In each area there is a Wild Country Expedition Panel with experienced volunteers able to advise on ventures being undertaken. The names and addresses of all the Panel Secretaries are published in the directory of the Spring edition of the *Award Journal*, on the Award's web site *www.theaward.org* and are available from Award Offices.

Advance notice, in duplicate, on the standard *Expedition Notification Form* must be given of all unaccompanied ventures in wild country areas including practice journeys. This notice, addressed to the Panel Secretary, must be given at **least six weeks in advance** (or four weeks in advance if a Panel Assessor is not required).

A notification reference number will be allocated to each qualifying venture and should be entered into the participants' *Record Books* following the successful completion of the venture. Award Groups are requested to inform the relevant Panel Secretary of any accompanied visits into the Panel area. These forms are available from Operating Authorities, The Award Scheme Ltd., *www.theaward.org* and Award Offices.

Acclimatisation

In order to adapt to the wild country environment, adjust to the routine of camp life and prepare themselves and their equipment, it is advisable for participants to spend forty eight hours in the area prior to the start of the qualifying venture. However, participants should always arrive in the wild country area the day before the start of the venture in order to meet with the Supervisor and Assessor. If camping, the base campsite should not be used by the groups as a campsite during the venture.

Ventures Outside the United Kingdom

For ventures outside the United Kingdom notice must be given to the Operating Authority **at least twelve weeks in advance** using the standard (blue) *Notification Form for Ventures Abroad*. The Operating Authority should accept responsibility for the safety of such ventures. Once the Operating Authority approves the venture it sends the information to the appropriate Award Office.

The Award allocates a notification reference number which should be entered in the participants' *Record Books* following the successful completion of the venture. For the Wild Country Panel in Bavaria the standard (green) *Expedition Notification Form* should be used.

Review

A debrief should take place immediately after the journey has been completed. It should be led by the Assessor and involve both the group and their Supervisor reviewing the outcomes of the venture. At this stage the Assessor may complete the section on the qualifying venture in the *Record Book*.

Once the participants have had time to reflect on the journey and its purpose they are asked to give a presentation or provide an account of their experiences. It is the responsibility of the participants to decide on its form and nature. It may be made individually or in a group and should be presented at an agreed time to the Assessor, Supervisor, Instructor or another person who has been involved in supporting the venture. This forms part of the final review when the appropriate Section in the participant's *Record Book* can be completed.

Variations to the Conditions.

In exceptional circumstances it may be necessary to vary the Award's conditions to meet the specific needs of certain individuals or groups. For example, it may be necessary to use barns, bothies or mountain huts instead of camping, or individuals may not be able to carry a full set of equipment, and require non-essential equipment to be pre-positioned at the campsites. Approval for such variations must be given by the appropriate person within the Operating Authority, as Operating Authorities have overall responsibility for monitoring the quality of the participants' experience and their safety.

For very experienced participants, approval may be given for unaccompanied out of season ventures by the appropriate person within the Operating Authority. If the venture takes place in wild country the plans should be agreed by the relevant Wild Country Panel and the Supervisor must hold the winter Mountain Leader Award or have equivalent experience.

Supporting Publications

The *Programmes File* contains useful information including the detailed Common Training Syllabus for each level of Award. Participants, Instructors, Supervisors and Assessors should also use the *Expedition Guide* and other relevant Award publications such as the *Exploration Resource Pack, Land Navigation - Route Finding Map and Compass* and *Playback – a guide to reviewing activities* as source materials and as a basis for their training programmes.

Explorations

Explorations enable participants to place greater emphasis on the 'discovery' element by reducing the 'journeying' requirement in the venture. Both types of venture must embrace both elements but the balance spent on each may vary.

The Relationship between Expeditions and Explorations

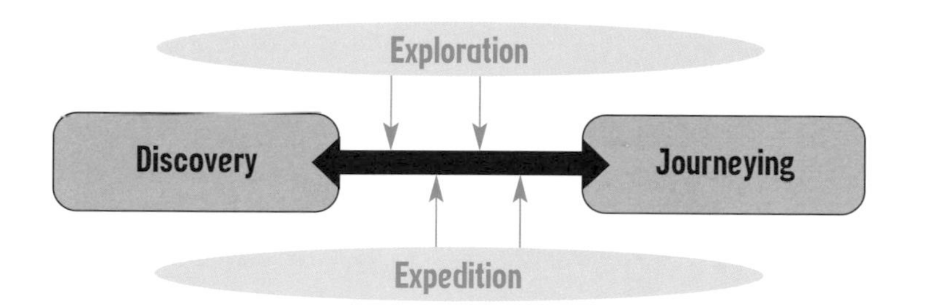

Conditions for Explorations

Explorations must take place within the context of an Expedition and must involve a minimum number of hours of journeying time spread over each day of the venture. All modes of travel used in Expeditions may be used for Explorations.

The same requirements and conditions apply except those which relate to distance or travelling time. Participants must complete the same preparation and training, including practice journeys.

The same campsite may be used on more than one night if the needs of the Exploration necessitate this. The site(s) of the Exploration and the campsite(s) should be remote to the extent that the group should feel the need to be self-reliant and dependent on its own resources.

At an early stage it is useful to find someone who is knowledgeable and experienced in the chosen field of interest and is willing to become the group's mentor. This person acts as an advisor, guide and friend and helps to derive the best value from the venture.

Detailed criteria for Explorations can be found in the *Programmes File* and *Expedition Guide*. The *Exploration Resource Pack* provides a wealth of information and guidance on the planning and preparation of Explorations.

Open Ventures

Open opportunities enable independent participants, and those unable to form a viable group, to complete their qualifying venture. These opportunities, usually at Silver and Gold levels, include a familiarisation and planning period followed by a supervised and assessed qualifying venture. All the necessary training and practice journeys must have been undertaken before a participant can take part.

Open Silver and Gold weeks are regularly advertised in *Award Journal* and on the Award's web site *www.theaward.org*

Other Adventurous Projects

Other Adventurous Projects are of an equally or more demanding nature than the normal Gold Expedition or Exploration but depart from some of the specified conditions. They provide participants with even greater scope for imagination and enterprise for their venture.

Although there is great scope for innovation, Other Adventurous Projects must still comply with the spirit and principles of the Expeditions Section i.e. an unaccompanied journey which has been planned and prepared by the participants where they are self-reliant and sufficiently remote from habitation to be dependent on their own resources.

Participants must submit an application outlining their plans, via their Operating Authority and Award Office, **in sufficient time to reach the Award Head Office at least 12 weeks prior to the date of departure.**

In giving approval for Other Adventurous Projects, the Award Office only confirms that the project is acceptable as a Gold qualifying venture in the Expeditions Section.

The Award cannot accept any responsibility concerning the suitability of the venture for the participants, safety aspects, the adequacy of the training or emergency procedures. These responsibilities must rest with the Operating Authority.

Before making their submission, participants should read the relevant chapter in the *Expedition Guide* which gives guidance on the information needed for a successful application.

Supporting Roles and Responsibilities

Operating Authorities are responsible for the safety and well-being of the participants and the approval of the Instructors, Supervisors and Assessors. Operating Authorities have activity procedures, which set out the training, experience and/or qualifications required for their Instructors, Supervisors and Assessors. Leaders must ensure that Operating Authority requirements are fulfilled.

Many Operating Authorities have local expedition teams able to support participants in undertaking their ventures.

The nature of self-reliant unaccompanied ventures places particular responsibilities on Instructors, Supervisors and Assessors. Whilst the Award does not insist on specific qualifications, Supervisors and Assessors are strongly recommended that, where suitable national qualifications exist appropriate to the mode of travel and administered by national governing bodies of outdoor pursuits, these should be obtained.

Detailed advice on instruction, supervision and assessment can be found in the *Expedition Guide* and the *Programmes File*.

Instructors

Instructors provide training in one or more aspects of the Common Training Syllabus which is outlined in the *Programmes File* and available on the Award's web site *www.theaward.org*

The safety and well-being of the participants is dependent on the quality of the training, as is the quality and enjoyment of the total expeditioning experience.

Training should be provided by those who have the necessary skills and experience. First aid training should only be given by an instructor approved by the Operating Authority.

The Expedition Instructor should plan training sessions to enable the participants to become increasingly self-reliant and dependent on their own resources. Training must be concerned with team building as well as with developing individual talents and resources within the team to strengthen the group as a whole. Regular reviewing sessions can enhance this.

Supervisors

All ventures, including practice journeys, must be supervised by a suitably experienced adult who accepts responsibility for the safety and well-being of the group on behalf of the Operating Authority. The Supervisor, who is the agent of the Operating Authority, must be satisfied that the participants are competent and equipped to undertake the planned venture.

Supervisors should be familiar with the aims, objectives, requirements and conditions of the Expeditions Section. They should be sufficiently experienced and competent in the mode of travel to be able to provide safe and effective supervision.

Groups undertaking their qualifying venture must not be accompanied except in exceptional circumstances, such as some water ventures, when closer supervision may be permitted. Contact should not be made with the group during the venture except for the needs of assessment and supervision. In certain circumstances, for safety reasons, it may be important that support from an adult should be quickly and easily available at night.

Supervisors should always carry with them all the relevant safety information which may be required. This will include the names, addresses and emergency contact numbers of the participants (usually their parents or guardian), the Assessor, a responsible person in the Operating Authority and Award Head Office.

During all qualifying ventures the Supervisor should be within or sufficiently close to the area of venture to render help within a reasonable time if an emergency should arise. For ventures in wild country or Explorations on the sea, coast and remote areas of marshland, the Supervisor must be based in the vicinity of the area where the venture takes place.

Ventures in estuaries or sheltered coastal waters may be supervised from a safety boat. The safety boat must be sufficiently remote from the participants to avoid restricting the group's sense of remoteness and self-reliance and yet be able to render assistance in an emergency within a reasonable period of time.

The Supervisor or Assessor should be aboard yachts in open sea areas but should not be involved in the skippering, crewing, navigation, control or management of the boat, except for reasons of safety. They should hold the RYA or DTp Yachtmaster Offshore Certificate.

Assessors

All qualifying ventures must be assessed by a competent adult who is either an approved Operating Authority Assessor or, if the venture is in wild country, an Assessor from one of the Award's Wild Country Panels. Assessors have three main functions:

- to ensure that the requirements and conditions of the Expeditions Section are fulfilled
- to advise on the safety of the venture – the ultimate responsibility rests with the Supervisor who is the agent of the Operating Authority
- to safeguard the interests of the Award

At Bronze level the Assessor should not have been involved in any of the training or instruction of the group

At Silver level the Assessor should be independent of the Award Group and at Gold level the Assessor must be independent of the Award Group and not associated with the group in any way.

For assessments taking place in a designated Wild Country Area an Assessor from the appropriate Wild Country Panel or from an Operating Authority should be used.

The Assessor should be accredited through the Award's Wild Country Assessor Accreditation Scheme. For details contact Award Offices.

RESIDENTIAL PROJECT

Aim of the Residential Project

To broaden young people's experiences through involvement with others in a residential setting.

The Principles

To introduce young people to some form of purposeful enterprise in the company of others who are not known to them.

Benefits to Young People

The Residential Project should give young people the opportunity to:

- **meet new people**
- **experience an unfamiliar environment**
- **build new relationships and show concern for others**
- **work as part of a team towards shared goals**
- **accept responsibility for self and others**
- **develop communication skills**
- **show initiative**
- **enjoy living and working with others**

Requirements

To undertake a shared activity or specific course in a residential setting away from home and in an unfamiliar environment.

Participants will normally require briefing or training prior to or during the residential period so that they are able to contribute fully and derive full benefit from the experience.

General Conditions

Where and What?

Residential settings may typically be in centres, youth hostels, sailing ships or camps. Staying with a family or 'home stays' are not generally acceptable.

The type of residential experience is to be the young person's own choice, freely made and without any financial gain.

The Project should provide opportunities for broadening interest and experience – it is the ideal opportunity to try something new. Under some circumstances, however, it may be related to existing interests or activities being followed in other Sections of the Award, but will be additional to the requirements for that Section. Practice journeys and qualifying ventures for the Expeditions Section cannot be regarded as a Residential Project.

With Whom?

In order to fulfil the objectives of the Residential Project, it is probably most beneficial for participants to join projects individually. Alternatively, only a small minority of those taking part should be known to the participant. To ensure that young people make new friends and build new relationships, this aspect is essential.

For How Long?

The project should normally take place over at least five consecutive days with at least four nights spent away.

In exceptional circumstances, and at the discretion of the Operating Authority, this commitment can be spread over two weekends provided that they involve at least four nights away within a twelve month period and the same activity is pursued.

Suitable Opportunities

Some participants may choose projects where the majority of participants are of their own age group whilst others may choose to be part of a small team working with young children or elderly people.

Residential opportunities can offer a range of challenges, but before making a choice, the main purpose must be clear. For example, physical activities can develop personal skills such as problem solving and a sense of achievement, whilst a drama course can improve communication skills and confidence.

With adequate planning and sufficient time allocated for reviewing and reflection, benefits and outcomes can be achieved through most types of Residential Project

Suitable opportunities generally fall into one of the categories listed below. Further examples can be found in the *Award Journal, Programmes File* and on the Award's web site *www.theaward.org*

- conservation or environmental work
- service to others
- activity based
- personal training

Preparation Prior to Attending

- discussion with the Award Leader or helper prior to making a choice will enable participants to think through the value of a particular opportunity for personal development
- the project must comply with the safety criteria of the Operating Authority and the requirements and conditions of the Award. Participants should seek guidance and approval from their Operating Authority before making a final commitment
- once the choice of Residential Project has been made, individual participants should contact the relevant organisation or course organiser to inform them of their wish for the experience to count towards their Award and to confirm further details
- before attending, each participant should identify a suitable assessor, approved by the Operating Authority, who will be in close regular contact throughout the period of residence
- check appropriate insurance is in place

The assessor should be briefed about the requirements and aims of the Residential Project and given a copy of the relevant *Sectional Leaflet*.

Assessment

On arrival at the venue, the participant should remind the course leader or instructor that the project will form part of their Gold Award. A meeting should be arranged with the assessor during and at the end of the project to review progress and discuss issues related to the experience.

Young people should be assessed on:

- personal standards
- relationships with others
- responsibility
- initiative
- development of skills
- knowledge and general progress

They should also have the opportunity to review the quality of their experience with their assessor or mentor.

The assessor should complete the *Record Book*. The participant may add their own comments if they so wish.

4

Chapter 4 Operating the Award

Operating the Award

Any group or individual in regular contact with young people may apply to an Operating Authority (see page 80 for further information on Operating Authorities) to run the Award. Groups must have an Award Leader to oversee the running of the Award.

The Award Programme can be operated in a variety of ways to complement existing activities and interests and to meet local needs and conditions.

4.1 Role of the Award Leader

To operate the Programme successfully and offer young people a comprehensive range of activities, a team approach is desirable with a designated leader undertaking the responsibility for co-ordinating the work of helpers and participants.

The Leader need not be involved with the detailed running of any particular part of the Award, but should ensure continuity, pooling of expertise, a sharing of responsibilities and the overall quality of the Award experience.

4.2 Responsibilities of the Award Leader

Some tasks can be delegated to helpers and participants.

To Operating Authorities

- liaise with the Award Officer of the appropriate Operating Authority
- obtain promotional and operational publications
- comply with the administrative, operational procedures and policies of the Operating Authority and the Award
- issue *Entrance Packs* and *Record Books* obtained from the Operating Authority
- understand the insurance arrangements of the Operating Authority and the Award
- forward completed *Record Books* to the Operating Authority for authorisation
- arrange the presentation of badges and certificates in discussion with the Operating Authority

To Participants

- discuss with participants their choice of activities
- record participants' progress through the Award
- help young people to continue the Award on relocation

- return Record Books to participants once Award has been validated
- obtain parental/guardian support and consent where appropriate

To Staff and the Community

- recruit, brief and arrange the training of helpers in accordance with Operating Authority procedures
- identify and, where appropriate, directly organise suitable activities in the community
- launch and promote the Award
- review financial arrangements

For Quality Assurance

- monitor, review and assess the quality of participants' experience through the Award using appropriate methods (peer review, one-to-one or group discussions, self-evaluation etc)
- keep up-to-date on Award developments through the Award Journal, web site, local networks and through conferences, courses and training events

4.3 Starting an Award Group

The following action plan outlines the main tasks involved in setting up an Award Group, although these may vary according to local circumstances.

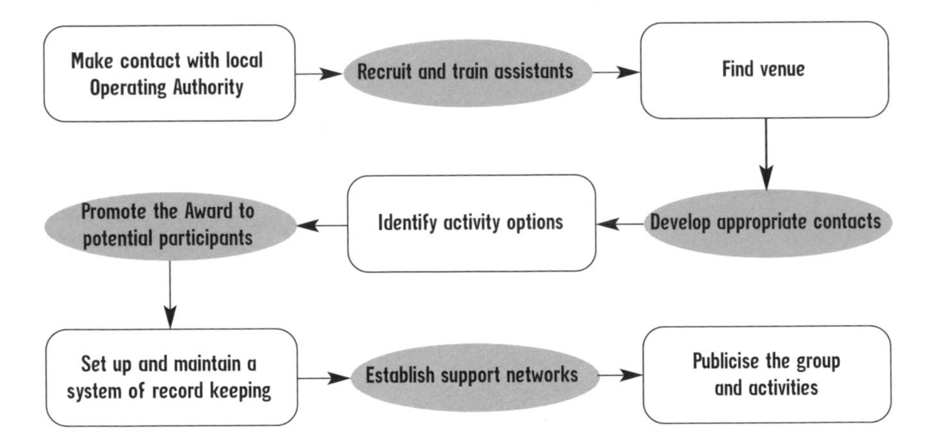

1. Make contact with the local Operating Authority and the Award Officer who can provide:

- information on the Operating Authority's procedures and channels of communication
- information on the local area and opportunities available for young people
- information on Operating Authority procedures and policies
- information on local resources including equipment, particularly for Expeditions
- supplies of Award publications
- a system for keeping records and administrative support
- contact with other Award users
- access to training courses

2. Recruit and develop assistants and helpers who have:

- a genuine interest in young people
- the ability to communicate
- a particular expertise they wish to share
- an empathy with young people
- an appreciation of their responsibilities to young people and the Operating Authority

3. Identify a venue which is accessible to young people which may be:

- a school or youth centre
- a business or commercial organisation
- an independent 'Open' Centre (including internet café, sports centre etc)
- anywhere young people like to meet

4. Develop contacts with local organisations which may:

- offer activities
- be a source of potential participants
- offer a source of helpers or volunteers
- provide equipment or materials
- sponsor events

5. Enrol young people who should:

- understand the challenge of the Award
- decide which level of Award to work towards
- complete an enrolment form
- obtain a Record Book and Entrance Pack
- decide on a personal programme

6. Promote the Award to young people by:

- using the Award's promotional material
- giving talks or presentations
- involving Award holders
- running an open or taster event

7. Plan and organise activities by:

- involving young people
- identifying people with appropriate skills
- delegating tasks and working as a team
- satisfying individual needs and aspirations
- utilising the resources of the community

8. Maintain accurate records by:

- keeping copies of enrolment forms and any activity sheets
- checking details are completed and entered in the *Record Books*
- explaining the purpose of the *Record Book* and *Entrance Pack*s
- obtaining the Operating Authority's approval of instructors and assessors
- adhering to the financial and administrative procedures of the Operating Authority
- monitoring and recording progress regularly
- forwarding Record Books to the Operating Authority for approval of Awards

9. Establish support networks including:

- parents and guardians of participants
- potential fundraisers and local business contacts
- influential members of the local community
- other Award Groups
- local Award Committees

10. Publicise the Award Group by:

- involving participants in organising events and displays
- using the local press, radio or internet
- publicising the achievements of the young people using all available resources and opportunities
- inviting local councillors and the business community to open evenings
- arranging Award presentation evenings

4.4 Instructing, Supervising, Mentoring and Assessing

The involvement of a number of volunteers prepared to devote their talents, enthusiasm and time to help young people discover the enjoyment of Award participation is a key ingredient to the successful operation of the Award.

A large volunteer base will increase the breadth of choices which can be offered to young people. The aim should be to seek a little help from as many people as possible rather than a great deal of help from just a few.

A personal approach to recruiting volunteers and helpers is more successful than a general call for help and this also helps target the resources and skills most required. Having secured the co-operation of individuals, it is important to sustain their interest and enthusiasm and to ensure that they fully understand their role.

Instruction, supervision and assessment should be undertaken by suitably experienced and, where appropriate, qualified people who are approved through the system used by the Operating Authority. This approval must be confirmed before a young person embarks on a particular activity.

With regard to older participants, these responsibilities may be carried out by a colleague or peer.

Seeking the advice of national associations, clubs and societies is recommended as a means of identifying qualified instructors.

The use of mentors within the Award is encouraged, particularly with regard to older participants who may feel less attracted to some Award Group environments. Mentors are individuals who support the participant in their progress through the Award, acting as a 'sounding board', encouraging reflection on progress, reinforcing key learning outcomes and further opportunities for development. Such individuals can also provide valuable support to young people who need particular encouragement.

Briefing and, where necessary, training for instructors, supervisors and assessors is essential and the appropriate *Sectional Leaflets* should always be provided together with a copy of any programmes which are being used for guidance. The basis of assessment is laid down in the detailed conditions for each Section in chapter 3. Further information can be found in the Award's *Programmes File* and on the Award's web site *www.theaward.org*

Expedition assessors operating in wild country (usually at Gold level) should be accredited through the Award's Wild Country Assessor Accreditation Scheme.

4.5 Empowering Young People

The Award encourages Operating Authorities and Leaders to involve participants individually, within their peer groups or through forums, in considering how best to use the Programme to address:

- the issues that affect their lives
- how the award is designed and delivered to help meet those needs
- how resources are allocated to support that process

4.6 Links With Other Programmes

The flexibility of the Award Programme enables it to be used in conjunction with programmes of many other partner organisations such as youth clubs, Scouts and Guides within higher and further education establishments, businesses and young offenders institutions. Activities followed through these organisations may also count for the Award, provided that the relevant conditions are fulfilled.

4.7 Support

For participants under the age of 18, it will normally be necessary to obtain parental/guardian consent, not only to satisfy the requirements of the Operating Authority but also to engage their interest and support. Parents and guardians can often help as instructors and assessors (or recruit others to do so), and provide equipment, transport and other facilities. Their support and encouragement is often instrumental in sustaining enthusiasm.

4.8 Award Holders

Award holders can give valuable assistance in helping others to gain Awards.

The *Award Link* also offers the opportunity for Award holders to remain in touch with the Award through the *Link* magazine, website and social and training events. Further information on *Link* can be found at *www.awardlink.org* or from Award staff.

4.9 Certificates and Badges

After the Award has been authorised, certificates may be presented with a miniature stickpin, badge or brooch for Gold participants, or with a pin badge for Bronze and Silver participants.

Sectional Certificates are available in each Section of the Bronze, Silver and Gold Awards. These may be issued at the discretion of the Award Leader, with the approval of the Operating Authority.

The certificates provide participants with tangible recognition as they progress through each Section of the Award. For young people who are unable to complete all Sections of the Award, these certificates provide recognition of their achievement. For the full Award, the *Record Book* must be authorised by the designated officer in the Operating Authority.

4.10 Award Presentations

Badges and Bronze and Silver Certificates should be presented locally by Operating Authorities as soon as is practicable after participants have completed their Awards.

Many Award Groups, Operating Authorities and Award Committees arrange presentations of Awards to give status to the achievements of all participants, and to provide an opportunity for local publicity. Invitations to participants should await confirmation of their Award.

Those who achieve the Gold Award are invited to a reception held at one of the Royal Palaces. When the date of the Gold Presentation is known (and this may be some time after the Award has been confirmed) an invitation will be sent to the Gold Award holder.

4.11 Publicity

Award Groups are instrumental in generating local publicity and attracting new entrants and volunteers. Publicity of, and for, the Award can be achieved by:

- celebrating young people's achievements in their local communities at presentation events and through the local media
- distributing information on when Award Groups meet
- promoting the activities and successes of local Award Groups, engaging the active support of local sponsors and key community figures

4.12 Access for All

There is sufficient choice and flexibility within the Award to enable all young people to access the Programme irrespective of resources, ability, religion or ethnic background.

Young people are encouraged to take responsibility for their Award. This includes making decisions on the suitability of choices made in terms of costs, venue, travel requirements, availability of a suitable instructor, supervisor and/or assessor and other resources.

However, it is recognised that some participants and groups may need added support and guidance to enable them to make informed choices.

Award Activities

It is usually Award activities rather than the cost of enrolment, which make the greatest financial demands on young people. There is sufficient flexibility in the Programme, for individuals to make choices which match their resources. Award participation frequently opens doors to subsidised activities and there are often local or national trusts which offer grant aid to individuals. Access to pools of equipment maintained by Operating Authorities or Award Committees can significantly reduce the cost of participation, particularly in the Expeditions Section.

Publications

An extensive range of Award operational and promotional materials is available free of charge. The Award Group should obtain a *Handbook, Programmes File* and *Expedition Guide*. These are available through Operating Authorities or from Award Scheme Limited.

Enrolment / Entry into the Award

Upon enrolling in the Award participants normally purchase an *Entrance Pack* and *Record Book*. which helps to support the cost of Award services, including the provision of Wild Country Panels, publications, advise, support, limited insurance cover and Gold Award presentations.

Communities

The Award Programme is flexible enough to be adapted to meet the needs of, and support participation by, the many communities within the United Kingdom.

Disability

Knowledge and understanding of the principles of the Award and the flexibility of the Programme are of paramount importance in ensuring that individuals with a disability are challenged within their capabilities. Where participants have learning difficulties or limited mobility, completion of a Section may take longer and require more training, practice, research, imagination and ingenuity on the part of both participants and helpers.

The Physical Recreation Section can also pose particular challenges for some participants, but there is a wide choice available and the list in this *Handbook* is not exhaustive. The activity undertaken should be based on the individual's ability rather than their disability.

The conditions detailed in the *Award Handbook* should generally be met, although it is possible to agree variations where a participant has a physical or sensory disability. These are probably more likely to be necessary for the Expeditions Section than for any other. Variations on the grounds of learning difficulties alone are not usually necessary, as there is sufficient flexibility of choice within the Award.

At all levels any proposed variations should be discussed with, and approved by, the Operating Authority. At Gold level the appropriate UK Award Office must be involved in the consultative process to ensure that participants receive effective guidance based on examples of good practice.

There are times when the Award requires its participants to work as a group. Guidance on forming the group should be given so that each member will be actively involved and challenged at a level relating to their personal capabilities.

Sectional certificates are available on completion of each Section and provide recognition of success. For those who find the Award unsuited to their own range of capabilities, or who fall outside the Award's age range, there are a number of other recognised regional and national Awards which may be more appropriate, e.g. The Gateway Award.

Additional guidance and information can be obtained from the appropriate UK Award Office.

Chapter 5 Operating Authorities and their Responsibilities

Operating Authorities and Their Responsibilities

Organisations, Local Authorities or other bodies concerned with the education, welfare or training of young people may apply to become licensed as an Operating Authority.

In order to obtain a licence, which is subject to review, Operating Authorities have to satisfy the Award that they understand the full implications of running the Award Programme. They have to be in a position to safeguard its aims and standards, to establish the necessary administrative framework to enable it to function and to ensure its continuity.

As part of the licence renewal process Operating Authorities should monitor the quality of the operation of the Award within their authorised Groups. Evidence of providing a quality experience for young people is necessary to support this process. Further information on possible methods of monitoring and evaluating performance can be obtained from Award Officers.

Operating Authorities will discuss with new Award Leaders, through their induction training, the range of services and support they provide, which includes those outlined in the *Operating Authorities Guide*.

Any young person wishing to participate must do so through an Operating Authority, either through an Award Group or as an independent participant.

Operating Authorities vary in size from national organisations, large companies and local authorities to individual establishments, such as independent schools and businesses. Most Award Groups operate under the umbrella licence of an existing larger Operating Authority, wherever this is practicable, in order to maximise the number of opportunities to network and pool resources.

5.1 Award Groups

The Programme's flexibility enables it to be operated in various settings. It offers the means of linking together a great number of organisations and individuals concerned with the personal development of young people. Most Groups are located at existing meeting points such as schools, higher or further education establishments, youth centres, workplaces or probation day centres. Using the Award as an added value component to complement existing training, education, supported study or extra curricular provision can assist the further development of young people and offer a form of accreditation.

5.2 Open Award Centres

Open Award Centres provide a facility for independent participants to become involved. The unifying principle of an Open Award Centre is that they operate an 'open door' policy to young people to participate fully in the Award. They provide ideal opportunities for effective personal and social development.

5.3 Independent Participants

Older participants may find it beneficial or preferable to undertake their Award independently i.e. not attached to a particular Award Group. Support for these participants can be achieved through use of the Award's Internet site, independent use of the *Handbook*, or contact with a mentor, possibly the Award Officer - by e-mail, phone or informal meetings to discuss and review progress.

5.4 Benefits of Operating the Award

Operating Authorities recognise that The Duke of Edinburgh's Award is a youth programme which enjoys high public recognition and acclaim.

- the Award provides an **'off-the-shelf'**, accessible, personal development programme geared to the development of the individual with an extensive range of support materials and advice from experienced Award staff
- three levels of Award and a **progressive approach** provide tangible evidence of success and effort on the part of young people
- the Award Group attracts a large number of **volunteers** who derive great satisfaction from sharing their enthusiasm, experience and skills
- operating the Award encourages the establishment of **community networks** and links. The Award has thrived as a result of the contribution of many voluntary and statutory agencies. These agencies are usually willing to assist any operator of the Award
- the Programme has a **value** which is recognised both nationally and internationally
- the Award is concerned with 'empowering young people to take greater responsibility for their own lives, to discover new talents, to advocate on behalf of others and to take positive action in the community' and, therefore, has a major contribution to make to the **youth work curriculum**
- as an **extra-curricular activity** in schools and colleges the Award can act as a value added component for enriching the personal and social development of pupils and enhancing a range of cross-curricular elements

- the sense of self-confidence, the problem-solving skills and the ability to work as part of a team are **valued by employers**, not only when recruiting staff, but also as a training opportunity for their existing workforce
- the Award is an effective means of working with disadvantaged young people and can support an Operating Authority on citizenship, social inclusion and community volunteering

Further information relating to the functions of Operating Authorities and advice concerning operational and administrative matters and insurance details are contained in the *Operating Authorities Guide.*

5.5 Supporting Organisations

Assisting Organisations

There are a large number of UK, national and international organisations who have pledged their support to the Award and are able to offer assistance in many specialist fields, such as producing new programmes, giving guidance on technical and safety matters and offering training courses to Award participants.

Further reference to appropriate bodies is made in the detailed conditions for each Section of the *Programmes File* and the Award web site *www.theaward.org*

Access Organisations

Many organisations work with young people in a particular interest area, such as sports or performing arts. Through the Access initiative, an Operating Authority can recognise the activity-providers as Access Organisations.

These organisations can issue inserts for *Record Books*, known as access credits, to young people who have completed the requirements for one Section of the Award Programme with them. The young people are not, at that stage, participants in The Duke of Edinburgh's Award, but they are given the option to approach an Operating Authority, enrol and then count the activities already signed up in the access credit by inserting it into their *Record Book.*

Young people may already be involved with an Access Organisation. There is no limit on the number of Access Organisations that may be approved by an Operating Authority. However, care must be taken to ensure that demand from young people to enter the Award does not exceed the opportunities available within associated Operating Authorities. Further details and information can be obtained from UK Award Offices.

In addition, a number of UK-wide or national organisations are approved by the Award Head Office as Access Organisations. These include organisations such as the Sail Training Association and Outward Bound. A list of these organisations is available on the Award's web site *www.theaward.org* and from Award Offices.

5.6 Training

The Operating Authority is responsible for identifying suitable learning opportunities for Award Leaders and helpers. This can take the form of meetings, courses, conferences and distance learning provided by the Operating Authority and/or the Award Office. The 'Over to You' Series can provide a basis for training.

Award training can be accredited both locally and UK-wide through frameworks such as the Open College Network. Operating Authorities may also provide opportunities to gain qualifications in youth work and outdoor activities. The Award accredits expedition assessors in wild country through its Assessor Accreditation Scheme.

Learning opportunities are publicised by Operating Authorities and Award Offices, and are advertised in the *Award Journal* and on the Award web site.

Chapter 6 Structure of the Award

6.1 The UK Framework

Operation

Responsibility for the operation of the Award is delegated under licence to Operating Authorities who are authorised to grant Awards (see page 80).

The Award is structured and delivered as follows:

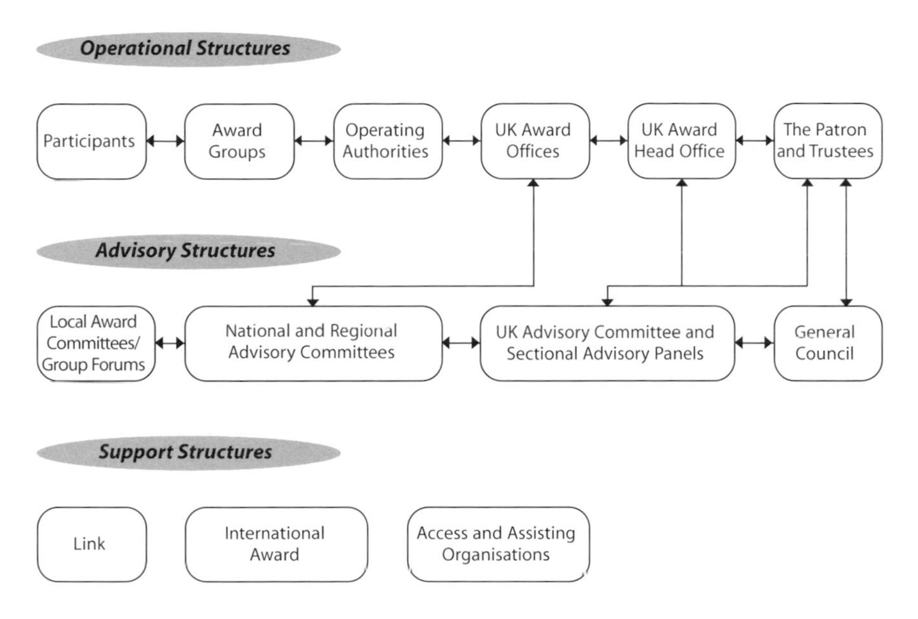

A Board of Trustees governs the Award and it determines the criteria and maintains the integrity and quality of the Award. A consultative and advisory framework, comprising the UK Advisory Committee, national and regional committees and Sectional Advisory Panels, advises the Trustees who may refer matters of policy to the biennial General Council.

The Award is administered on behalf of the Trustees by Award staff in Head Office and eleven offices throughout the UK, who deal with matters of overall policy and central administration.

The Award gives a clear indication of standards through its licence to Operating Authorities.

To support Operating Authorities in meeting their objectives, Award staff:

- administer and monitor the delivery of the Award throughout the UK
- co-ordinate the development of policy through the Advisory Committees, Advisory Panels and General Council
- produce operational, promotional and training materials
- approve and issue Operating Authority licences to organisations
- ensure Award conditions and programmes are appropriate and relevant in a rapidly changing society
- arrange Gold Award Presentations
- provide information, advice and assistance to Operating Authorities, Award Groups and Assisting Organisations, including the provision of the Wild Country Panels
- actively promote the Award to all potential users and initiate new developments
- liaise and establish working relationships with local, national and UK government, Operating Authority Award Officers together with other Award users, and act as a focus of information for enquiries
- organise courses and conferences to share good practice, promote new developments and standardise quality of delivery

6.2 Award Committees

Award Committees and Group Forums can be set up at the discretion of Operating Authorities and the Award Officer. They can provide a valuable consultative framework to assist with the promotion and development of the Award in a particular area.

6.3 The International Award Association

The Award now operates in almost 100 countries. While the title may vary, the underlying philosophy and basic principles of operation are the same.

The International Award Association is the governing body for all countries throughout the world who offer the Award, including the United Kingdom. Further information can be obtained from:

The International Award Association
Award House
7-11 St Matthew Street
London SW1P 2JT

Tel: 020 7222 4242
Fax: 020 7222 4141

www.intaward.org

Chapter 7 Publications

Publications

A wide range of operational and promotional material is available from the Award's mail order and distribution service, the Award Scheme Ltd (ASL) (see page 94 for contact details). Details may be found in the catalogue and order form published annually and available from ASL, Award Offices or Operating Authorities.

The main items for operating and promoting the Award are listed below:

7.1 Support Materials

Award Handbook - the principal operational publication - essential for all those operating the Award.

Programmes File a loose-leaf folder containing detailed programmes for each Section. Regular updates are featured in *Award Journal* and in an annual update pack, available from ASL.

Over to You Series – a series of training resource booklets to assist trainers in planning and running training courses at all levels.

Expedition Guide - detailed guidance and advice on all aspects of expedition training and qualifying ventures at all levels and for all modes of travel.

Sectional Leaflets - a set of leaflets outlining the conditions for each of the Sections of the Award. They give essential guidance for all instructors, supervisors and assessors.

Award Journal - the Award's magazine published in January, April and September, is free to Operating Authorities. It contains features and editorials on areas of special interest and a calendar of training events and conferences, items of operational importance and changes to the conditions and requirements of the Award and information on new publications.

Quest for Quality – a guide for Operating Authorities on the benefits of a quality approach to operation and delivery.

Promotional leaflets, posters and videos an extensive range available.

Publications are also available covering the operation of the Award in a range of contexts such as schools, further education, higher education, business, working with young offenders etc.

Additional information for the Expeditions Section is also available:

Exploration Resource Pack - loose-leaf pack giving ideas, information and advice for the purpose of Explorations and Expeditions.

Land Navigation Route-Finding with Map and Compass – detailed guidance on finding your way and using a map and compass in various terrains.

7.2 The Duke of Edinburgh's Award Logo

The Duke of Edinburgh's Award name and logo are registered trade and service marks and should only be used by those authorised to do so. All licensed Operating Authorities are authorised to use the logo and they in turn can authorise Award Groups, Local Award Committees and Expedition Panels acting under their auspices. Any other individual, group or organisation wishing to use the logo should obtain written permission in advance from Award Head Office in Windsor. The guidelines set out below should be followed.

- the logo should be used in full and should never be redrawn or adjusted manually or by computer
- once approved, the organisation or group name must always be shown in conjunction with the logo
- the design can be printed in black or two colours (blue and red only as detailed below)
- if printing in two colours, the blue is Pantone 281 and the red is Pantone 199. If printing in the four colour process, the blue is a mix of 110% Cyan, 72% Magenta and 38% Black. The red is 100% Magenta and 65% Yellow
- the design can be printed in white out of a solid dark blue
- it can also be printed with the words reversed out (white) from a blue solid with the cypher and flashes in red

Detailed guidance on how best to apply the design, along with artwork for reproduction, is available from Award Head Office.

7.3 Glossary of Terms and Roles

There are a range of key roles in the operation of the Award. The following descriptions should be helpful in clarifying these:

Access Organisations
An organisation through which a young person can complete one section of the Award prior to enrolment.

Assessors
Appropriately qualified, experienced or accredited individuals, approved by the Operating Authority, who confirm whether participants have fulfilled the conditions and requirements of a particular Section of the Award as specified in the *Award Handbook*.

Award Leader
Co-ordinates, monitors and advises young people in their Award Group.

Award Officer
The person designated by the Operating Authority to be responsible for all aspects of Award operation by and within the organisation.

Helpers
Assists the Award Leader in the administration, organisation and operation of a particular aspect of the Award.

Instructor
Approved by the Operating Authority, the instructor helps young people to acquire knowledge of and improve their skills in a particular activity, in order to comply with the requirements specified in the *Award Handbook*.

Mentor
An individual who supports a participant in progressing through the Award, acting as a 'sounding board', encouraging reflection on progress, reinforcing key learning outcomes and identifying further opportunities for development.

National Governing Body
Any organisation or body of people, with responsibility for setting activity standards, programmes, achievement levels and qualifications.

Operating Authority
Any authority, organisation or other body concerned with the education, welfare or training of young people that holds a licence to operate The Duke of Edinburgh's Award.

Participant

A young person who has enrolled with an Operating Authority to undertake the Award Programme.

Supervisors

In the Expeditions Section the supervisor is responsible to the Operating Authority for the safety and well-being of the young people during their practice and qualifying ventures.

In other Sections, the supervisor is responsible for supporting young people by arranging the necessary briefing and review sessions and offering advice.

UK Award Offices

There are eleven Award Offices throughout the UK in addition to the UK Head Office.

UK Award Office Contact Details

- Northern Ireland: 28 Wellington Park, BELFAST BT9 6DL
  Tel: 028 9050 9550 Fax: 028 9050 9555 E-mail: nireland@theaward.org
- Scotland: 69 Dublin Street, EDINBURGH EH3 6NS
  Tel: 0131 556 9097 Fax: 0131 557 8044 E-mail: scotland@theaward.org
- Wales: Oak House, 12 The Bulwark, BRECON, Powys LD3 7AD
  Tel: 01874 623086 Fax: 01874 611967 E-mail: wales@theaward.org
- East Midlands: c/o Chilwell Comprehensive School, Queens Road West, Beeston, NOTTINGHAM NG9 5AL
  Tel: 0115 922 8002 Fax: 0115 922 8302 E-mail: eastmid@theaward.org
- West Midlands: 89-91 Hatchett Street, Newton, BIRMINGHAM B19 3NY
  Tel: 0121 359 5900 Fax: 0121 359 2933 E-mail: westmid@theaward.org
- South East: 10 Station Road, CHERTSEY, Surrey KT16 8BE
  Tel: 01932 564800 Fax: 01932 564788 E-mail: southeast@theaward.org
- South West: Court Gatehouse, Corsham Court, CORSHAM, Wiltshire SN13 OBZ
  Tel: 01249 701000 Fax: 01249 701050 E-mail: southwest@theaward.org
- North East: Martime Chambers, 1 Howard Street, NORTH SHIELDS, Tyne and Wear NE30 1LZ
  Tel: 0191 270 3000 Fax: 0191 270 3007 E-mail: northeast@theaward.org
- North West: Churchgate House, 56 Oxford Street, MANCHESTER M1 6EU
  Tel: 0161 228 3688 Fax: 0161 228 3960 E-mail: northwest@theaward.org
- East: 17 Lower Southend Road, WICKFORD, Essex SS11 8ES
  Tel: 01268 571393 Fax: 01268 562060 E-mail: east@theaward.org
- London: 7th Floor, Therese House, 29-30 Glasshouse Yard, LONDON EC1A 4JN
  Tel: 020 7253 5544 Fax: 020 7253 5224 E-mail: london@theaward.org
- Head Office: Gulliver House, Madeira Walk, WINDSOR, Berkshire SL4 1EU
  Tel: 01753 727400 Fax: 01753 810666 E-mail: ops@theaward.org
- Award Scheme Ltd: Unit 18/19 Stewartfield Industrial Estate, Off Newhaven Rd, EDINBURGH EH6 5RQ
  Tel: 0131 553 5280 Fax: 0131 553 5776 E-mail: enquiries@aslhq.demon.co.uk